AUNT
FREDDIE'S
PANTRY

Clarkson N. Potter, Inc./Publishers
DISTRIBUTED BY CROWN PUBLISHERS, INC., NEW YORK

AUNT FREDDIE'S PANTRY

SOUTHERN-STYLE PRESERVES,
JELLIES, CHUTNEYS, CONSERVES,
PICKLES, RELISHES, SAUCES...
AND WHAT GOES WITH THEM

by Freddie Bailey

Text with Mardee Haidin Regan
Photographs by Brigitte Lacombe
Foreword by Lee Bailey
A Word from Liz Smith

Published by Clarkson N. Potter, Inc., One Park Avenue, New York, New York 10016, and simultaneously in Canada by General Publishing Company Limited

Manufactured in the United States of America
Designed by Rochelle Udell
An earlier version of this book was previously published in different form under the title *Freddie Bailey's Favorite Southern Recipes*

Library of Congress Cataloging in Publication Data
Bailey, Freddie.
    Aunt Freddie's pantry.
    Previously published under title: Freddie Bailey's Favorite southern recipes.
    Includes index.
    1. Jelly. 2. Jam. 3. Cookery (Relishes) 4. Sauces.
I. Regan, Mardee Haidin. II. Title.
TX612.J4B35 1984   641.8'1   83-27006
ISBN 0-517-55300-7

10 9 8 7 6 5 4 3 2 1

First Edition

Contents

Two of my favorite people: my great-granddaughter Leanne and my nephew Lee.

Foreword

The first recollection I have of my remarkable aunt Freddie is that of a pretty young woman (just how young I only now realize) riding a green bicycle laden down with bundles of slipcovers. On the warm summer morning I remember, my mother had driven over to see her sister-in-law and had overtaken her just as she was peddling into the driveway. Freddie's husband and my father were brothers, and luckily when she and my mother met they liked each other on sight—over the years becoming more like real sisters than sisters-in-law. I had been brought along to play with my cousin (Freddie's daughter, also named Freddie), who was but a few months older than I, and, like me, destined to be an only child—and whom I absolutely adored. This adoration was accepted in a royal sort of way by the younger Freddie, or rather in the way of a cat to which you pay too much attention. After all, I *was* younger—and a boy.

That year the country was still deep in the Great Depression, not exactly a time for high spirits and hopes, but as she was to do several times before ultimately settling in Natchez, Mississippi, for good, Freddie was busily making a home for her small family. She had painted the walls of their little house white and the floors a dark eggplant color—which she did in every house she ever lived in that I knew of—had sewn muslin curtains to which she had added string fringe, which she knotted herself, filled the flower beds with simple hearty flowers, and was even trying to coax wild buttercups to grow along the bank of a ditch. This day the slipcovers were finished and she was happily putting the final touches on her decorating job. My mother and Freddie shared an interest in houses, so I suppose mother had gone over to visit and to take a look at the completed rooms. Anyway, the memory seems pertinent because it is filled with clues to Freddie's personality. Expressed in that boundless energy and forthright enthusiasm was her faith in herself and the future. She somehow always managed to do all those things she had set herself to without any seeming strain; and then to add to what for some people would be a full-time job, she spent enough afternoons at the country club to become a more than passable golfer, and became the owner (and manager) of an antique shop, which later evolved into a successful clothing store. She also liked to go fishing with her husband, who lived to celebrate their golden wedding anniversary with her, and to cook. The cooking was always as straightforward as everything else about her. Good food, lots of it, and all done with gusto and ease.

I have another memory from several years later. The same pretty young woman is standing in a house full of shouting and giggling girls, all eight or nine years old, with tears rolling down her cheeks—and laughing in spite of them. We had all gone down to

"Shady Nook" for the day, where Freddie and her husband had rented a cabin full of beds so that Freddie could chaperon a group of her daughter's friends for a week's stay (of swimming, eating, screaming, and telling ghost stories for the girls and undoubtedly lots of cooking and coping for her). When it came time for all the adults (and me) to leave, she just couldn't stand to see us go and started to cry and then to laugh at herself for being so sentimental. It seems a moment ago—but Freddie will soon be eighty. Thank heaven she hasn't changed.

I think Freddie's book speaks for itself, but I wanted to speak a little for Freddie. And to say God bless you, you sweet human being.

Lee Bailey, nephew, age fifty-five

A Word from Liz Smith

In some parts of the world a sign of "class" is the time one eats the evening meal. The general dining hour of the civilized haut monde is between 8:00 and 9:00 P.M., and the Spanish, who find even this barbarous, eat at 11:00 or midnight. (I suppose only we "proles" like to eat early, because we've had a hard day's work and want to get it over with so that our time is free for other projects—sleeping, quarreling, watching TV, making love, and that most wonderful and fatal of fattening happenings, preparing for the late night snack.)

The eating early syndrome produced a joke in the parts of Mississippi and Texas whence my countrified forebears hail. It goes, "What time's dinner ready?"

Answer: "Six o'clock—five-thirty if it's ready!"

When I contemplate the culinary wonders of Freddie Bailey's fertile and creative sleight of hand and mind, I forget all about the years I spent striving for upward and social mobility. I want to push the dining hour up even earlier. And earlier. And earlier.

Regardless of the hour, I can't think of anything that would signify more fun to me, or be looked forward to more heartily, than knowing I was going to sit down for lunch or dinner at one of Freddie's groaning tables in Natchez, where the Tot, Teen & Mom Shop in her famous Victorian house occupies only a part of her busy and productive life. Dreaming up ways to make us all fat and happy seems to me to be her greatest gift. And to heck with people who like to nibble lettuce leaves and cook with white grapes.

I see Freddie Bailey these days stirring the pots for her widely heralded pepper jelly as I first saw her stoking the fires for an outdoor clam and lobster boil on Long Island at the Bridgehampton house of her nephew Lee Bailey. Freddie is an experimental adventurer—willing to try anything. A dedicated cook—dedicated to the joyous outcome. A natural artist of life—being a perfectionist who is not picky. A jolly southern belle-turned-loving matriarch—in charge and brimming with know-how and joie de vivre.

I am an inveterate reader, if not necessarily a user, of cookbooks. I can't think of another one that has given me the pleasure of this one. To open it to any page is to feel one's salivary glands tingle. Freddie Bailey's vision of how we can be what we eat is unique, funny, and appealing, just like its creator.

She makes me want to say, "Four-thirty—if it's ready!"

I love this picture of my mother in "regimental garb," and that's me, below, at age two.

Introduction

I was raised on butter, molasses, and biscuits in a place called Ruston, Louisiana. The town was founded by my granddaddy, Robert E. Russ, on plantation land he donated to start it. I still visit Ruston from time to time, and one thing hasn't changed at all since I was a girl: They grow the biggest, sweetest, juiciest peaches I've ever eaten.

I don't recall too much about my girlhood in Ruston, though certain images are still as plain as day. I remember summer nights at my grandmother's house, sleeping under a mosquito bar (net) that hung over my bed, and I remember cold winter nights at home when we'd all sit around the wood fire until bedtime, and my daddy would wrap a hot brick in a towel and put it in my bed so my feet weren't cold. I remember my soft, warm feather bed, and most of all, I remember our kitchen at home. Mother was a wonderful cook and the kitchen was the hub of the house, with a big old wooden table to sit around. Everything she cooked always smelled so good. One thing never changed at our house: My father wanted biscuits three times a day—at breakfast, lunch, and supper. I don't think he liked bread at all, but there was no question about his feelings for biscuits.

Once, when I was nine or ten, Mother was sickly and she knew Daddy's biscuits had to get made. So she sent me down to the kitchen and told me to measure out the flour and buttermilk and put them on a tray with the other ingredients. I brought the tray up to her bed and she talked me through my first biscuit making—the first of many batches I was to make.

I went to college in Ruston and met a man named Herbert Bailey. We married, and sixty-three years ago, Freddie Jimerson became Freddie Bailey. And what a life we led. Like me, Herbert loved a party. He was a wonderful dancer and it seems we were always having fun, surrounded by crowds of friends. With all that we had abundant good food; my pantry always served me well.

Our entertaining was casual—not at all stiff or formal. My husband liked to cook up pots of his favorite stew, sauce piquante, whenever we decided to throw an impromptu party. It was a good choice because he could stretch it out by adding a bit more meat or some extra vegetables. With it, we'd serve the relishes, pickles, and chutneys that I'd put up, as well as biscuits or corn bread with my preserves on top. I always kept a supply of pimiento and cheese on hand; it turned crackers or bread into hors d'oeuvre or sandwiches. At our parties, we drank a little and ate a lot.

During the earlier part of our married life, we lived in several places—Bunkie, Ville Platte, and Opelousas, Louisiana. You see, my husband helped manage his father's chain of movie theaters, so we moved to whatever town had a picture show that needed management. My husband loved to fish, and in Grand Isle, Louisiana—way down on the Gulf—we had a fishing camp. For about half of every month, we were there eating seafood, catching crabs, and fishing. Why, there were times when you could catch two speckled trout at a time. We'd just roll the fillets in cornmeal and fry them. They were sooo good. Sometimes, I would go down to talk to the fishermen when they came in off the boats. I'd give them a beer while we talked, and often they'd all pitch in and fill my Igloo cooler with fish. I'd give them pepper jelly in return. Other times, when we had company, we'd run down when the shrimp boats came in and buy 50 pounds of shrimp, then lug them home and sit on the screened porch, drinking beer and pulling their heads off. Sounds terrible, but even that was fun.

No matter where we lived, we ate well. When crawfish were in season, I cooked with them until I couldn't look at them anymore. During hunting season, we dined on wild duck and quail and tiny, sweet doves. And, always, we entertained. There was never a time that I couldn't toss together a big green salad and work up some sort of meal from what I had on hand. At family occasions, one favorite was the homemade, hand-churned vanilla ice cream that was such a delicious treat. We all—children and adults—took turns at the hand crank—usually the children first, when the mixture was barely frozen, and the adults later, when the crank got tougher and tougher to turn. It was such a special happy time for everyone. If we had them, we'd add Ruston peaches to the ice cream. And if we didn't, my pantry was always stocked with good things to spoon over the top.

Ever since I was a young woman, it seems I've had a knack for doing business. Once I taught some friends how to knit and ended up in the yarn business. Another time, more recently, I needed some pecans to make candy and ended up in the mail-order pecan business. The same thing happened with antiques. Each new business seemed to grow into another one. It infuriated my husband because it took me away from our fishing and playing time. But he didn't stop me. He waited—impatiently—until I closed my shop each night.

Herbert and I were living in Tallulah, Louisiana, when I heard that Natchez was *the* place to be. We decided to take a look and found the beautiful house (built in 1890) that has been my home for the past thirty-six years. I have my children's and women's clothing store here, and it's where I sell my hot pepper jelly. But out back, behind the house, is my favorite place—my jelly kitchen.

I've been making pepper jelly there for years and years. But I've been in the mail-order business for only the last fifteen. My nephew, Lee Bailey, thought my jelly was so good and so unique that he strongly urged me—fairly forced me, in fact—to start selling it. He told me to have some pretty labels made, put the jelly up in nice little jars, and sell it in my shop. Well, I did as he told me to do and I've sold jelly to people in every state. Now I put up about four hundred jars a week.

I'll never forget my first, most exciting, mail-order

experience. A lady from California wrote the Natchez police department asking them to help her locate the lady who made hot pepper jelly. Well, of course, they knew it was me she wanted—the station is only a few blocks from my house. You can't imagine how tickled I was that she went out of her way to find me and my jelly. Since then, more and more people have liked my jelly. Around Christmastime, my busy season, I hire several high school youngsters to help me make the Santa Claus gift boxes for my jelly and help with the packing and shipping. That leaves me more time to get out there in my jelly kitchen. It's where I never let myself think about troubles or bad things. I mean it when I say I want good thoughts and love to go into the jelly. It's like good luck. I've had a happy, happy life, and the main reason for it is that I've had such great help—from my family and friends.

When I was a little girl, every night before I said my prayers, my mother would ask, "Now, Sister, what did you do nice for somebody today?" Or she'd say, "Did you speak with an old person?" You see, she just wanted me to do something thoughtful, something that would help.

I hope this book is helpful to you today. I've filled it full of good things that my friends and family have always enjoyed. Things you can make and keep for when you need to take them off your pantry shelf and enjoy them. I hope you do.

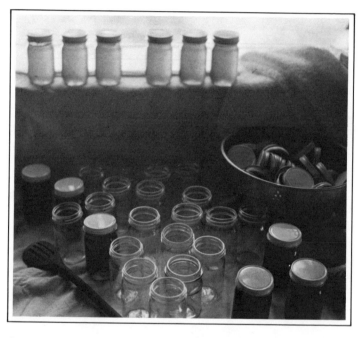

My canning jars look so pretty all in a row by the window.

Some Thoughts About Canning

No matter what you're planning to preserve, it's always smart to start fresh. Use fresh, unbruised fruit or vegetables that are in peak condition. And always, always take the time to properly sterilize your canning jars. I like to use Ball or Kerr brand canning jars with new metal lids and screw tops. I wash them in hot, soapy water and rinse well. Then I put the jars and lids in a large kettle with water to cover, bring the water to the boil and boil for 5 minutes. I use tongs to transfer them to drain, upside down, on a tray covered with paper towels in a low (200°) oven.

When I preserve foods, I strictly control the quality of what goes into them and the cleanliness of the kitchen where they're prepared. I frequently do not bother to process my foods in a boiling water bath, because I add enough sugar or vinegar to ward off most bacteria. I like to fill the jars to ¼ inch from the top, wipe the rims clean, cap and seal each one, then turn the jars upside down to ensure that the seal is good.

If you want to process canned goods, use a wide, deep kettle and put a rack on the bottom. Place capped jars on the rack, so that the jars don't touch each other or the sides of the kettle. Add hot water to cover the jars by about 2 inches and boil for the amount of time recommended in each recipe. Cool jars overnight at room temperature. Next day, remove the screw caps and check that the lids are tightly sealed.

I'm not a fussy person, but my kitchen is certainly filled with the things I love.

Preserves and Jellies

PEAR PRESERVES

Pear preserves are soothing to eat with breakfast toast on a hot summer morning. If you like, add a stick of cinnamon and cook it with the pears.

16 cups peeled, sliced pears
2 pounds (4 cups) sugar
Juice of 1 lemon
2 cups water

Place the pears, sugar, and lemon juice in a large pot and add 2 cups of water. Cook over moderate heat until the pears are tender and the syrup is thick.*

Ladle the preserves into hot, sterilized jars and seal. Process for 5 minutes in a boiling water bath, if desired.

MAKES 8 TO 10 HALF-PINTS

*I like to add about 3 drops of red food coloring because it makes the pears look more appetizing.

I have a beautiful fig tree growing right in my back-yard, but for some reason, it didn't bear last year. I had to advertise for figs in the newspaper and the result was wonderful. I had dozens of little boys bringing me my favorite kind of figs. They're brown and about the size of a big pecan. These preserves are my nephew Lee's favorite. He sends them to all his friends in New York City.

Fig preserves are good on hot Buttermilk Biscuits (page 63) with lots of butter and also on Homemade Ice Cream (page 66). When my daughter was little, I used to keep a jar of fig preserves mixed with peanut butter, so there were always the makings for a fast sandwich.

10 pounds small figs, stemmed
5 pounds (10 cups) sugar
3 lemons, seeded and thinly sliced

Wash the figs in cold water. Place them in a heavy pot with the sugar and add just enough water to cover the sugar and keep the figs from sticking. Add the lemon slices and cook over moderate heat until the syrup is thick and the fruit is tender.* Skim off the foam that comes to the top.

*To make a thicker fig conserve, add chopped pecans and seeded lemons (juice, pulp, and peel) that have been chopped in a food mill, grinder, or food processor.

When the juice has become a syrup, divide among hot, sterilized half-pint jars and seal. Turn the jars upside down to ensure a perfect seal. Process for 5 minutes in a boiling water bath, if desired.

If I need to go out somewhere, I just turn the fire off and finish the figs later. The resting time helps the figs—they puff up while I'm gone.

MAKES ABOUT 16 HALF-PINTS

A huge paper plant shades the window of my kitchen.

This easy pineapple marmalade is a winterime staple—it's so good when fresh fruit is hard to get. It's very versatile—I serve it with ham and smoked meats, use it as a filling between layers of a cake, or spread it all over the bottom of a baking pan for my daughter Freddie Gee's favorite pineapple upside-down cake.

2 20-ounce cans crushed pineapple in
  unsweetened juice
1½ cups packed dark brown sugar
1 tablespoon lemon juice
1 cinnamon stick, broken in half
¼ teaspoon freshly grated nutmeg

In a heavy saucepan, combine all the ingredients. Cook, stirring occasionally, over moderate heat until the liquid is thickened, 30 to 40 minutes.

Ladle into hot, clean jars and set aside to cool. Cap tightly and refrigerate. Will keep about a month.

MAKES ABOUT 6 HALF-PINTS

QUICK BERRY PRESERVES

My nephew, Lee, inspired me to make these quick preserves. He hates to can foods but loves the strawberries that are abundant in the summer on Long Island, where he lives. The method is borrowed from him; I do it with either strawberries or blackberries— or a mix of both. Blackberries tend to be tarter, so you might need more sugar.

1 quart berries, such as strawberries or
blackberries
1 cup sugar
1 teaspoon fresh lemon juice

Clean the berries, remove the stems, and halve them (quarter them if large). In a heavy saucepan, combine the berries with the sugar over moderate heat. Bring to the boil, stirring occasionally, and reduce the heat to low. Pour in the lemon juice. Cook until the fruit is soft but not mushy, about 10 minutes.

Using a slotted spoon, divide the berries among the jars. Continue cooking the liquids until reduced by half. Pour over the berries and set aside to cool. Cap tightly and refrigerate. Will keep about a month if you can keep them around that long!

MAKES 3 TO 4 HALF-PINTS

These hot pepper cranberry preserves came about as a pleasant surprise—when I forgot to add the gelling agent and decided to use my hot pepper jelly in place of the sugar. It just couldn't be easier to make. Try it with roast turkey for Thanksgiving or as a chutney with curried dishes.

2½ cups Hot Pepper Jelly (page 22)
  2 quarts cranberries

In a heavy pot, bring the jelly and 3 cups of water to the boil over moderately high heat. Add the cranberries and cook over moderate heat until the skins burst. Pack just the berries into hot, sterilized jars and continue cooking the syrup until it thickens. Pour it over the berries and seal. Process for 5 minutes in a boiling water bath, if desired.

MAKES 8 TO 10 HALF-PINTS

W ild plum, quince, mayhaw, crab apple, grape, or dewberry jellies are never a failure when made this way. I failed a few times before getting the right proportions. You might want to try these fruits without the Sure-Jell, since they are naturally high in pectin and acid. (Or give it a try with cranberries, gooseberries, lemons, or loganberries.)

2 quarts strained juice from cooked fruit
2 boxes Sure-Jell powdered fruit pectin
5 pounds sugar

Wash the fruit and remove the blossoms and stems. Do not core or peel. Place a large quantity of the fruit in a large pot and add water to cover. Cook over low heat until mushy, 3 to 4 hours, adding water as needed. Pass the fruit and juice through a jelly bag (or a colander lined with several thicknesses of dampened cheesecloth) into a pot. Measure the juice.

In an enameled or stainless-steel pan, heat 2 quarts of the juice to the boil and add 2 boxes of Sure-Jell. Stir well and let return to the boil. Dump in 5 pounds of sugar and stir until it dissolves. Let come to the boil again. Remove the pot from the heat and let set for 5 minutes. Skim off any white foam that comes to the top. Pour into half-pint jars. I like to pour the jelly into a pitcher to avoid spilling the liquid on the jars.

I never double this recipe.

MAKES 10 HALF-PINTS

I suppose I am most known for my hot pepper jelly. People seem to love it, and I love making it for others. The jelly is delicious with cream cheese on crackers or pumpernickel bread—just put a colorful dab on top. And it's good with ham, turkey, and lamb—or on sandwiches.

   2 *to 3 small green bell peppers*
   3 *to 4 hot red or green peppers*
6½ *cups sugar*
1½ *cups cider vinegar*
   2 *3-ounce pouches or 1 6-ounce bottle*
      Certo liquid fruit pectin
      Red or green food coloring (optional)

Wear rubber gloves to seed and coarsely chop the bell and hot peppers. Place the bell peppers in a blender or food processor and purée until liquefied. (If you need to, add 1 tablespoon of the vinegar to the pepper—just to moisten for easier blending.) You should have about ¾ cup. Purée the hot peppers until liquefied. You should have ¼ cup.

In a large pot, combine the 1 cup of puréed peppers with the sugar and vinegar over high heat. Bring to the boil and add the Certo. Add food coloring if you are using it. Bring to the boil again and pour the jelly into a pitcher. Pour into half-pint jars and seal.

MAKES ABOUT 7 HALF-PINTS

PEPPER JELLY TARTS

These tarts are so tasty and good. I always used to serve them at my bridge parties or at light luncheons. They're an ideal way to show off your homemade hot pepper jellies!

½ cup plus 2 tablespoons (5 ounces)
   cream cheese, cut into small bits
¼ pound (1 stick) unsalted butter, cut
   into small bits
1 cup all-purpose flour
   About ¾ cup Hot Pepper Jelly
   (page 22)
1 egg, lightly beaten

In a bowl, cut the cream cheese and butter into the flour until it forms a uniform mixture. Shape the dough into a ball—it will be rather sticky and wet. Wrap it in plastic and refrigerate for at least 1 hour or overnight.

Preheat the oven to 350°.

On a heavily floured board, roll out the dough about ¼ inch thick. Cut with a 2-inch round cutter. Spoon a scant teaspoon of pepper jelly in the center of each round. Fold over and press the edges together with a fork. Continue until all the dough is used. Brush the tops and seams with the beaten egg and bake until lightly browned, 15 to 20 minutes.

MAKES ABOUT 2½ DOZEN

My home at 400 South Commerce Street in Natchez.

Chutneys and Conserves

PEACH CHUTNEY

I use this same recipe to make apple chutney and pear chutney. I like to serve it with duck and game dishes.

- 5 *cups peeled, chopped, and stoned peaches*
- 2½ *cups tightly packed brown sugar*
- 1½ *cups golden raisins*
- ½ *cup chopped crystallized ginger*
- 1 *clove garlic, minced*
- 1 *lemon, seeded and chopped*
- ¼ *cup brandy or bourbon*
- 2 *cups cider vinegar*
- 1½ *teaspoons salt*
- 1 *cinnamon stick*

In a large pot, combine all of the ingredients. Bring to the boil over moderate heat, stirring frequently. Reduce the heat to a simmer and cook until the fruit is tender. Remove the cinnamon stick, ladle the chutney into hot, sterilized jars, and seal. Process for 15 minutes in a boiling water bath, if desired.

MAKES 6 HALF-PINTS

GOOSEBERRY CHUTNEY

Gooseberries are underrated in America. They make up into a terrific chutney—one that my nephew, Lee, likes to use in his steamed puddings.

   2 *pounds gooseberries*
   1 *large onion, finely chopped*
1¾ *cups tightly packed brown sugar*
   2 *cloves garlic; minced*
   ½ *teaspoon yellow mustard seed*
1½ *cups raisins*
   1 *teaspoon ground ginger*
   1 *teaspoon salt*
   1 *teaspoon whole allspice*
   ½ *teaspoon cayenne pepper*
2½ *cups white vinegar*

In a large pot, bring all of the ingredients to the boil over moderate heat. Reduce the heat to low and simmer, stirring occasionally, until thick. Ladle into hot, sterilized jars and seal. Process for 5 minutes in a boiling water bath, if desired.

MAKES ABOUT 6 HALF-PINTS

CRANBERRY GINGER CHUTNEY

G inger makes such a difference when cooked with cranberries. I like to serve this chutney with brisket and also with game and game birds. My granddaughter-in-law, Anne, serves it every Christmas alongside smoked meats.

2½ *quarts cranberries*
 ½ *cup finely chopped green bell pepper*
1½ *cups raisins*
 2 *cups granulated sugar*
 2 *cups tightly packed brown sugar*
 1 *cup chopped crystallized ginger*
 3 *cups cider vinegar*
 ½ *teaspoon salt*
 ½ *teaspoon whole cloves, ½ teaspoon whole allspice, and 1 cinnamon stick, tied in a double thickness of cheesecloth*

In a large pot, bring the cranberries, bell pepper, raisins, sugars, ginger, vinegar, salt, and bag of spices to the boil over moderate heat. Reduce the heat to low and simmer, stirring frequently, until the color darkens and syrup becomes very thick, 1½ to 2 hours. Remove the bag of spices and ladle into hot, sterilized jars; seal. Process for 5 minutes in a boiling water bath, if desired.

MAKES 8 HALF-PINTS

SPICY PEAR CHUTNEY

There's nothing quite like a good pear. People bring me their excess fruit, and I trade them for my hot pepper jellies. This recipe works equally well if you make it with apples. It's good with baked ham and wild duck. Yield and cooking times will vary, depending on the varieties of pears (or apples) you choose and how small you cut the fruit.

8 *pounds fresh pears—peeled, cored, and cut into quarters, slices, or chunks*
8 *cups tightly packed brown sugar*
6 *cups cider vinegar*
2 *teaspoons whole cloves*
1 *cinnamon stick*

Combine all of the ingredients in a large pot over moderate heat. Bring to the boil and cook until the fruit is tender. Spoon the fruit into hot, sterilized jars, pour in the liquid to within ¼ inch from the top, and seal. Process for 15 minutes in a boiling water bath, if desired.

MAKES ABOUT 8 PINTS

APPLE TOMATO CHUTNEY

In the fall of the year my thoughts turn to this chutney because it uses the end of the tomato crop and the beginning of the crisp apple crop. My family thinks it's just great alongside some slices of Pepper Jelly Glazed Ham (page 51).

    8 cups peeled, cored, and chopped apples
      (about 6 apples)
 4½ cups peeled and chopped tomatoes
    2 cups coarsely chopped onions
    1 red bell pepper, seeded and chopped
    1 hot pepper, seeded and chopped
    1 clove garlic, minced
    3 cups tightly packed brown sugar
    2 cups cider vinegar
  ½ cup chopped stem ginger
  ½ cup orange juice
    1 tablespoon salt
    1 teaspoon ground cinnamon
    1 teaspoon ground allspice

In a deep enameled or stainless-steel pot, bring all of the ingredients to the boil over moderate heat. Reduce the heat to moderately low and cook until the apples are tender and the mixture is very thick, 1½ to 2 hours. Ladle into hot, sterilized jars and seal. Process for 5 minutes in a boiling water bath, if desired.

MAKES 10 HALF-PINTS

I was born in Ruston, Louisiana, and I've never tasted peaches as good as the ones from there. They're sweet and juicy—just perfect for this easy conserve. Spread it on slices of pound cake or lemon bread or use as a filling for little open-faced tarts.

7 *cups peeled, sliced ripe peaches (about 5 pounds)*
4 *cups sugar*
3 *cups golden raisins*
2 *lemons, seeded and thinly sliced*
1 *orange, seeded and thinly sliced*
1 *teaspoon whole cloves, 1 teaspoon whole allspice, and 1 cinnamon stick, tied in a double thickness of cheesecloth*
1½ *cups chopped pecan pieces*

In a large pot, bring the peaches, sugar, raisins, the lemon and orange slices, and the bag of spices to the boil over moderate heat. Cook for about 25 minutes, stirring frequently, until the mixture is somewhat thickened. Add the pecans and stir to distribute them. Remove the bag of spices and ladle the conserve into hot, sterilized jars. Wipe the rims and seal. Process for 5 minutes in a boiling water bath, if desired.

MAKES 8 HALF-PINTS

APPLE, PEAR, AND LEMON CONSERVE

The sweet and spicy flavors in this conserve seem right at home with smoked turkey or fried chicken. You might want to spread some on top of hot Buttermilk Biscuits (page 63), directly out of the oven. Use whatever apples and pears are in season when you make this recipe.

4 cups peeled, cored, and chopped apples
4 cups peeled, cored, and chopped pears
  Grated peel and juice of 4 lemons
2 cups golden raisins
4 cups sugar
1 cinnamon stick
¼ cup water

In a large pot, combine all of the ingredients over moderate heat. Stir together and cook slowly for 30 to 40 minutes, until thick. Ladle the mixture into hot, sterilized jars, leaving ¼ inch of headspace, and seal. Process for 5 minutes in a boiling water bath, if desired.

MAKES 8 HALF-PINTS

I always think happy thoughts when I'm in my jelly kitchen.

Pickles and Relishes

BREAD 'N' BUTTER PICKLES

To make these pickles, I use whatever kinds of cucumbers that anybody brings me. They're easy and delicious and one of my family's favorites. The flavor of these pickles improves with age.

- 8 *cups thinly sliced cucumbers*
- 2 *onions, thinly sliced*
- ½ *cup salt*
- 3 *cups sugar*
- 2 *cups cider vinegar*
- 4 *green bell peppers, seeded and finely chopped*
- 2 *teaspoons celery seed*
- 2 *teaspoons turmeric*
- 1 *cinnamon stick*

In an enameled or stainless-steel pot, combine the cucumbers, onions, and salt and let stand overnight.

Next day, drain and discard the liquid. Add the sugar, vinegar, bell peppers, celery seed, turmeric, and cinnamon and bring to the boil. Cook for 20 minutes. Pack into hot sterilized jars and seal. Process for 15 minutes in a boiling water bath, if desired.

MAKES 4 PINTS

M y old neighbor used to specialize in making the prettiest pale green sour pickles. He grew his own pickling cucumbers and always was generous about sharing them with me. He loved these garlic pickles that I made with his sours. (If you don't have a handy source for sours, you can use bottled ones from the supermarket.) These pickles will spark up the flavor of any baked fish or fish salad. They are also delicious deep-fried (see next recipe).

- 25 *large sour pickles, cut into ¼-inch slices*
- 5 *pounds (10 cups) sugar*
- 1 *1.12-ounce box pickling spice*
- 5 *cloves garlic, sliced*
- 2 *cups tarragon vinegar*
- 1 *cup olive oil or other vegetable oil*

Using an earthenware crock, stainless-steel or enameled pot, or a large glass jar, make a layer of pickles and top it with a liberal amount of the sugar, pickling spice, and garlic slices. Continue layering, alternating rows, until all of the ingredients are used. Cover with cheesecloth and let stand for 3 days, stirring occasionally with a wooden spoon. Add the vinegar and oil and stir thoroughly. Let stand for 10 days before packing into hot, sterilized jars and sealing.

MAKES 10 TO 12 PINTS

Several Natchezians—Sally Ballard, Weeta Colbank, and George and Anne Eyrich—own a restaurant, The Cock o' the Walk, overlooking the Mississippi River. Their fame has come from their perfect fried catfish and these unusual deep-fried dill pickles. They gave me permission to share the recipe with you. I'd serve these pickles with just about anything, but smoked ham is probably my favorite.

    Vegetable oil, for deep-frying
 1 *egg, beaten*
 1 *cup milk*
 1 *tablespoon Worcestershire sauce*
 5 *to 6 drops Tabasco sauce*
 2 *cups plus 1 tablespoon all-purpose flour*
    Salt and pepper
10 *medium dill or garlic pickles, sliced*

In a deep-fat fryer, heat the oil to 350°.

In a shallow bowl, combine the egg, milk, Worcestershire, Tabasco, and the 1 tablespoon of flour. Season with salt and pepper.

In another bowl, combine the remaining 2 cups flour with salt and pepper to taste. Dip the pickle slices first into the egg mixture, then into the flour. Dip it into the egg for a second time and into the flour again—two full turns each. Fry until golden brown, drain on paper towels, and serve hot.

SERVES 4

SUMMER SQUASH AND ZUCCHINI PICKLES

Pretty yellow summer squash and green zucchini taste so good and they seem to grow like weeds. Remember, the smaller the squash, the tastier it will be. I save all the small ones for pickling. If you like, you can substitute Jerusalem artichokes for the squash; just use brown sugar and add four red hot peppers.

   8 *cups sliced yellow squash or zucchini*
   2 *large onions, thinly sliced*
   4 *medium red or green bell peppers,*
     seeded and sliced into rings
     Salt
   2 *cups cider vinegar*
   2 *cups sugar*
   2 *teaspoons yellow mustard seed*
   2 *teaspoons celery seed*

In an earthenware crock or a stainless-steel, glass, or enameled container, arrange a layer of the squash, onions, and peppers and salt the layer liberally. Continue adding layers and salt. Cover and set aside for 1 hour. Drain off the liquid but *do not rinse.*

In a large pot, bring the vinegar, sugar, mustard seed, and celery seed to the boil over moderately high heat. Add the vegetables and bring back to the boil. Count to 10; remove from heat. Ladle into hot sterilized pint jars, fill to ¼ inch from the top, and seal. Process for 5 minutes in a boiling water bath, if desired.

MAKES ABOUT 6 PINTS

I soak these sliced green tomatoes in pickling lime because it acts as a firming agent—the slices hold their shape much better after this treatment. Serve these pickles with old-fashioned pimiento and cheese sandwiches or chicken sandwiches.

- 1 *cup pickling lime (calcium hydroxide)**
- 7 *pounds green tomatoes*
- 2 *quarts cider vinegar*
- 5 *pounds (10 cups) sugar*
- 1 *1.12-ounce box pickling spice, tied in a double thickness of cheesecloth*

In an earthenware crock or large glass jar, dissolve the pickling lime in 1 gallon of water. Wash the green tomatoes and slice them ¼-inch thick. Soak the slices in the lime overnight.

Next day, wash the tomato slices several times; try not to break the slices. Place the tomatoes in a large pot and add the vinegar, sugar, and pickling spice. Bring to the boil over moderate heat, reduce the heat to low, and cook until tender, about 10 minutes. Remove the bag of spices, pack in hot sterilized jars, and seal.

MAKES 8 TO 10 PINTS

*Available at most drugstores.

I love chow chow. As you see from the yield of this recipe, I make a large amount of it at one time because it seems silly to do less. This is an old, old recipe—I do it exactly the way my mother did. It seems we always had these ingredients around. She used to serve chow chow to company at lunch. I like it on hamburgers, hot dogs, and barbecued meats.

24 *green tomatoes, chopped*
12 *medium green bell peppers, seeded and chopped*
10 *medium onions, chopped*
 2 *large heads of cabbage, shredded*
 2 *cups salt*
 3 *quarts white vinegar*
 1 *cup yellow mustard seed*
¼ *cup celery seed*
 2 *tablespoons whole allspice*

In a large earthenware, glass, or stainless-steel container, combine the tomatoes, peppers, onions, and cabbage. Dissolve the salt in 2 quarts of water and pour it over the vegetables. Let stand overnight.

Next day, drain the vegetables through a colander; *do not* press down on the vegetables. Discard the liquid.

In a large kettle, combine the vinegar, mustard seed, celery seed, and allspice. Add the vegetables and bring to the boil over moderate heat. Reduce the heat and cook gently for 10 minutes.

Fill hot, sterilized jars with a mixture of the vegetables, spices, and liquid. Turn the jars upside down to ensure a tight seal. Process for 15 minutes in a boiling water bath, if desired.

MAKES ABOUT 30 PINTS

BEET PICKLES

These beet pickles won't stay around your house too long—they tend to get eaten very quickly. Serve them with lunch, dinner, or anytime as a tasty snack.

4 quarts small beets, washed, leaves
* removed, and stems cut to within 1 inch*
2 cups cider vinegar
2 cups sugar
1 cinnamon stick
6 whole cloves

Cook the beets in water to cover for 15 minutes. Remove the root end and stem end, and slip off the skins. Cut into ¼-inch slices.

In a large pot, bring the vinegar, sugar, cinnamon, and cloves to the boil and cook for 15 minutes. Divide the beets among hot, sterilized jars and pour in the vinegar mixture to within ¼ inch of the top; seal. Process for 30 minutes in a boiling water bath, if desired.

MAKES 16 HALF-PINTS

My family loves this corn relish so much that it's hard to keep on hand. You can serve it just anytime at all—it's so versatile, it goes with almost everything. My nephew, Lee, likes to serve it alongside steamed greens (beet, turnip, or kale) sprinkled with vinegar.

20 ears of corn
¾ cup salt
2½ cups sugar
 1 1.12-ounce tin dry mustard
 1 tablespoon turmeric
 2 quarts white vinegar
 1 medium cabbage, sliced (about 3 cups)
1½ cups chopped green bell pepper
1½ cups chopped sweet red pepper
 6 large onions, chopped
 1 4-ounce jar pimientos, drained and chopped
 4 red hot peppers, seeded and chopped
 6 to 8 celery ribs, chopped (about 2 cups)

Cut the corn off the cobs. In a large pot, combine the salt, sugar, dry mustard, turmeric, and vinegar. Bring to the boil over moderate heat. Add all of the vegetables, reduce the heat, and simmer for 45 minutes.

Pack into hot, sterilized jars and fill with the liquid, leaving ¼ inch of headspace, and seal. Process for 15 minutes in a boiling water bath, if desired.

MAKES ABOUT 10 PINTS

This relish is popular at my house, since it's as good with sandwiches as it is with meats. I love it with a plain roast chicken or as a picnic condiment. I always have it on hand at my place on Lake Concordia.

7 *pounds ripe tomatoes, peeled and chunked*

6 *tart apples (such as Granny Smiths), peeled, cored, and chunked*

2 *large onions, finely chopped*

3 *sweet red peppers, seeded and chopped*

2 *sweet yellow peppers, seeded and chopped*

2 *cups cider vinegar*

1 *cup sugar*

2 *teaspoons salt*

In a large pot, combine all of the ingredients and cook over moderately low heat, stirring frequently, until hot. Reduce the heat to low and simmer, stirring occasionally, until the mixture becomes thick and fragrant, at least 15 minutes or more depending on the size of the chunks. Ladle into hot, sterilized jars and seal. Process for 15 minutes in a boiling water bath, if desired.

MAKES 8 PINTS

The shiny tools of my "trade"—pots, ladles, and pitchers.

Sauces

SPICY RUM-BUTTER SAUCE

This sweet sauce is particularly good on Warm Gingerbread (page 67). I also spread it on pound cake or any day-old cake.

¼ pound (1 stick) unsalted butter,
    softened
¾ cup sifted confectioners' sugar
2 tablespoons rum
1 teaspoon ground cinnamon
½ teaspoon freshly grated nutmeg

In a bowl, cream together the butter and sugar. Slowly add the rum and stir to incorporate it. Stir in the cinnamon and nutmeg. Spoon the mixture into a clean jar or crock and refrigerate. You need to let this set awhile to allow the flavors to develop. Before serving, let come to room temperature, until the texture is soft and smooth.

MAKES ABOUT 1 CUP

I f you have a taste for brandy, you'll like this sauce. It's good over Homemade Vanilla Ice Cream (page 66), custard, or sliced fruit. You can substitute bourbon or scotch if you wish.

  2 *egg yolks*
  ¾ *cup sugar*
  3 *tablespoons brandy, or more to taste*
  1 *cup heavy cream, whipped*

In a bowl, beat the egg yolks and sugar well. Add the brandy and whipped cream and mix thoroughly. Chill for at least 3 hours before serving.

MAKES ABOUT 2½ CUPS

PRALINE SAUCE

I like to start with a layer of ice cream and top it with a layer of this praline sauce and then continue layering the two of them in a parfait glass. Then I top that with whipped cream and it's heavenly.

2 cups molasses
⅓ cup boiling water
⅓ cup tightly packed brown sugar
1 cup chopped pecan pieces

Combine all of the ingredients in a saucepan and bring to the boil over moderate heat. When the mixture boils, remove it immediately from the heat. Pour into small, hot, sterilized jars and let cool. Cover and store in the pantry, or the refrigerator if you prefer it chilled.

MAKES ABOUT 4 HALF-PINTS

This caramel syrup is as homey as can be and couldn't be easier to make. It's quite good on breakfast waffles, Buttermilk Flapjacks (page 62), or a creamy egg custard.

1 cup sugar
1 cup boiling water

In a heavy saucepan, cook the sugar over very low heat, swirling the pan constantly while the sugar melts to a golden brown. You should not stir it; the sugar will caramelize by itself. Add the boiling water and cook over high heat for 3 to 4 minutes, until it is the consistency of maple syrup. You can flavor it with rum or add chopped pecans, if you like.

MAKES 1 CUP

CREAMY CARAMEL SAUCE

This thick caramel sauce makes a great ice-cream
sundae. Warm it up and it could challenge hot
fudge any day.

2 cups sugar
2 tablespoons unsalted butter
1 cup molasses
1 5⅓-ounce can evaporated milk
1 tablespoon vanilla extract

In a heavy saucepan, bring the sugar, butter, molasses, and milk to the boil over moderate heat. Off
heat, stir in the vanilla. Pour into half-pint jars and
store on your pantry shelf; refrigerate after opening.

MAKES ABOUT 2 HALF-PINTS

My hot mustard sauce is so good on anything that requires mustard—especially on a smoked ham or a brisket sandwich, which I make from leftovers.

    4 *ounces (1 large or 2 small cans)*
      Coleman's dry mustard
    1 *cup sugar*
    1 *cup cider or distilled white vinegar*
    2 *eggs*

Combine all of the ingredients in a blender or food processor and mix until smooth. Transfer the mixture to the top of a double boiler and cook over simmering water until thick. Spoon into a jar and refrigerate before serving. Will keep a long time, at least 6 months.

MAKES ABOUT 2½ CUPS

Y ou can use this barbecue sauce two ways: Either mix in the oil that comes to the top when you cook this sauce and brush meat or chicken with it, or do what I do and brush them with just the oil (which will have absorbed all those good flavors) and serve the thick tomatoey sauce separately with chunks of French bread to dip it in.

- 1 cup full-flavored vegetable oil (preferably peanut)
- 2 cups chopped celery
- 2 cups chopped onions
- ½ cup chopped green bell pepper
- 2 cloves garlic, minced
- 1 cup cider vinegar
- 1 teaspoon dry mustard
- 1 35-ounce can peeled tomatoes with their juice

In a large saucepan, heat the oil over moderate heat. Sauté the celery, onions, bell pepper, and garlic until tender, about 10 minutes. Add the vinegar, dry mustard, and tomatoes with their juice, breaking the tomatoes up with a wooden spoon. Cook over low heat for at least 30 minutes, until thick and flavorful. Refrigerate if not using at once. Will keep at least a month.

MAKES ABOUT 4 CUPS

In my jelly kitchen at the back of the house, the door is always open.

What Goes with Them

PEPPER JELLY GLAZED HAM

I buy the tastiest smokehouse hams, cooked in the southern style, and then heat them up and do my own thing with them. Naturally, I like to glaze them with my hot pepper jelly.

> 1 ready-to-eat ham (it may be smoked
> or otherwise processed)
> Whole cloves (optional)
> 1 cup Hot Pepper Jelly (page 22)

Preheat the oven to 375°.

Since the ham is cooked, all it really needs is reheating and glazing. Remove the rind from the ham and trim away all but a thin layer of fat. Score the fat and stud with cloves, if desired. Place the ham on a rack in a roasting pan.

In a small saucepan, melt the hot pepper jelly over low heat. Brush the entire ham with the liquid jelly. Bake, brushing frequently with the jelly, until the ham is heated through. Slice the ham and serve it with Hot Mustard Sauce (page 48).

W hen my husband and I had the duck camp in Grand Isle, Louisiana, we frequently prepared wild duck this way. Wild ducks have very little fat—they're mostly meat and wholly delicious. Spicy Pear Chutney (page 28) makes a nice accompaniment.

1   *wild duck*
    Salt
    Pepper
1   *medium onion, peeled*
2   *tablespoons unsalted butter*
1   *cup dry sherry*
½   *pound mushrooms, thinly sliced*
1   *teaspoon Worcestershire sauce*
3   *drops Tabasco sauce*
¼   *cup finely chopped parsley*

Season the duck with salt and pepper. Place the onion in the cavity.

In a heavy roaster or casserole, melt the butter over high heat until it is very hot. Brown the duck on all sides. Add the sherry and reduce the heat to low. Cook slowly for 5 minutes, turning often and basting with the sherry. Add the mushrooms, Worcestershire, Tabasco, and parsley. Cover and cook, basting frequently, for up to 30 minutes more, depending on desired degree of doneness.

Transfer the duck to a carving board and discard

the onion from the cavity. Meanwhile, reduce the cooking liquids over high heat to make a brown gravy. Cut the duck into serving pieces and place on a hot platter, accompanied with wild rice or buttered toast. Pass the gravy in a gravy boat.

SERVES 2

My daughter, Freddie, and me, as a young matron.

Brisket is my nephew Lee's favorite dinner. Though a plain-cooked pot roast suits him just fine, I like to cook it this way, with my barbecue sauce. I braise it a day ahead of time and finish cooking it outside on the grill or inside, in the oven. The initial braising creates a tasty gravy, which I set aside to put on hot leftover brisket sandwiches. Serve with any of my pickles and relishes.

   1 *tablespoon vegetable oil*
3½ *pounds brisket of beef*
  ⅓ *cup water*
  3 *large onions, chopped*
  3 *cloves garlic, minced*
     Salt
     Pepper
     Barbecue Sauce (page 49)

Preheat the oven to 350°

In a large heavy roaster, warm the oil over moderate heat. Sear the brisket on all sides until browned, about 5 minutes per side. Set the meat aside.

Add ⅓ cup water to the roaster and cook over moderately high heat, scraping up the brown bits that cling to the bottom. Add the onions and garlic and toss them in the liquid.

Transfer the brisket to the roaster and season it generously with salt and pepper. Cover and roast for

40 minutes. Turn the meat over and season with additional salt and pepper. Cover and roast for 1 hour more. Remove the brisket to a large sheet of foil. Set the gravy aside for another use.

Stir the barbecue sauce until well mixed and coat the brisket generously on all sides. (I like to really soak it with the sauce.) Wrap the meat in the foil, adding more sheets of foil to seal the package. Refrigerate overnight.

If finishing the cooking in the oven, preheat it to 350°. Place the wrapped brisket on the grill or directly on the oven rack and cook until tender when pierced with a fork, 1 to 1½ hours. Slice and serve with additional barbecue sauce on the side.

SERVES 6 TO 8

My husband loved to prepare this dish—we served it at countless parties—made with chicken or whatever meat or seafood was at hand. Experiment with it—add herbs and spices to suit your family's taste. This sauce freezes well and can be kept on hand at all times. Try it accompanied by Hot Pepper Cranberry Preserves (page 20), Chow Chow (page 38), or Green Tomato Pickles (page 37).

1 *cup vegetable oil*
2 *frying chickens, cut into serving pieces*
1 *cup coarsely chopped onion*
2 *cups coarsely chopped celery*
1 *green bell pepper, seeded and chopped*
⅔ *cup all-purpose flour*
1 *1-pound can Italian-style peeled tomatoes*
1 *8-ounce can tomato sauce*
½ *pound mushrooms, halved or quartered*
2 *bay leaves*
2 *cloves garlic, minced*
1 *tablespoon hot pepper sauce or more to taste*
1 *tablespoon fresh lemon juice*
   Salt and freshly ground black pepper
2 *tablespoons chopped green onion*
   (scallion) tops
2 *tablespoons chopped parsley*
12 *stuffed green olives, sliced*

In a heavy casserole or covered roaster, heat the oil over moderately high heat. Working in batches if necessary, add the chicken pieces and cook until browned on all sides, 5 to 10 minutes. Remove the chicken and set aside.

Add the onion, celery, and bell pepper to the hot oil and cook until lightly browned, 10 to 15 minutes. Remove with a slotted spoon and set aside.

Add the flour to the remaining oil and cook, stirring constantly, until the roux darkens to a deep brown shade, 15 to 20 minutes.

Stir in the tomatoes, tomato sauce, mushrooms, bay leaves, garlic, hot pepper sauce, lemon juice, and 4 cups water. Mix well and season liberally with salt and pepper. Add the reserved chicken and vegetables and bring to the boil. Reduce the heat to low and simmer for 2 hours, adding additional water, if necessary.

Stir in the chopped onion tops, parsley, and olives and serve hot over rice or pasta.

SERVES 8 TO 10

I don't know how anyone could dislike this venison. It's so good when I make it this way, on stovetop. Since the venison is very lean, you have to add the fat yourself—salt meat is perfect. Like any strong-flavored meat, venison needs a nice strong chutney to go with it—try my Cranberry Ginger Chutney (page 27) or Peach Chutney (page 25).

1 *4- to 5-pound venison roast*
1 *cup cider or distilled white vinegar*
3 *cloves garlic, halved*
  Salt
  Cayenne pepper
6 *pieces (each about ½ inch by 3 inches) salt meat (salt pork)*
  All-purpose flour
3 *tablespoons bacon drippings*
1 *cup finely chopped onion*
1 *cup finely chopped celery*
½ *cup finely chopped green bell pepper*
½ *pound mushrooms, sliced*
½ *cup dry red wine*

Place the roast in a pot just big enough to hold it. Add the vinegar and enough water to cover. Set aside for 3 hours. Discard the liquid, rinse the roast in fresh water, and pat dry.

Stick the point of a knife in the roast and wiggle

it around to make a hole. Make 5 more holes and plug each of them with a piece of the garlic, some salt, cayenne, and a piece of salt meat. Lightly dredge the roast in flour.

In a heavy pot or casserole, melt the bacon drippings over moderate heat. When hot, brown the roast on all sides. Add the onions, celery, and bell pepper and cook until the vegetables are tender, about 10 minutes. Add the mushrooms, red wine, and 2 cups of water. Cover, reduce the heat to low, and cook until the meat is tender, 2 to 3 hours.

SERVES 8 TO 10

Dove hunting is very popular in these parts, and I do love these sweet little birds. Every fall, my grandson Dee goes dove hunting. He cooks them this way, and I provide the Hot Pepper Cranberry Preserves (page 20) to go with them.

12 *doves, cleaned*
    Salt and pepper
    All-purpose flour
¼ *cup vegetable oil*
 1 *medium onion, finely chopped*
 3 *ribs celery, finely chopped*
 3 *cloves garlic, minced*
 3 *cups boiling water*
½ *pound mushrooms, sliced*

Season the doves with salt and pepper and dredge them lightly with flour. In a large cast-iron skillet or pot, heat the oil over moderately high heat. Brown the doves on all sides and remove them from the pan.

Reduce the heat and add the onion, celery, and garlic. Sauté until softened, about 10 minutes.

Add the doves, breast side down, and pack them closely together. Pour the boiling water over and add the mushrooms; stir well. Reduce the heat to low, cover the pan, and simmer, stirring frequently, until the doves are tender when pierced through the thickest part of the meat, 5 to 10 minutes. Remove the doves and boil the sauce until quite thick.

SERVES 4 TO 6

My granddaughter, Denise, loves this pie, and she doesn't even like sweet potatoes very much. It's delicious with a scoop of Homemade Vanilla Ice Cream (page 66) on top.

FILLING

- 2 cups mashed, cooked sweet potatoes
- 6 tablespoons unsalted butter, softened
- 2 eggs, beaten
- 1/3 cup granulated sugar
- 1 teaspoon vanilla extract
- 1/2 teaspoon cinnamon
- 1/2 teaspoon freshly grated nutmeg
- 1/4 cup evaporated milk
- 1 9-inch deep-dish pie shell, partially baked

TOPPING

- 3 tablespoons unsalted butter, melted
- 1/2 cup tightly packed light brown sugar
- 1/3 cup all-purpose flour
- 2/3 cup finely chopped pecans

Preheat the oven to 350°.

In a bowl mash together the sweet potatoes and the softened butter. Add the eggs, sugar, vanilla, cinnamon, nutmeg, and evaporated milk and stir well until smooth. Pour into pie shell; and smooth the top.

In a small bowl, combine the melted butter, brown sugar, flour, and pecans. Stir to blend; the mixture will be crumbly. Sprinkle topping over the pie.

Bake the pie on a cookie sheet 25 to 35 minutes.

OLD-FASHIONED BUTTERMILK FLAPJACKS

I f your family is like mine, they'll love these light, fluffy flapjacks. When the mood strikes me, I like to add chopped pecans or banana to the batter. My grandson Dempsey always requests these for his birthday breakfasts, topped with my homemade jellies or preserves.

1½ cups all-purpose flour
1 tablespoon sugar
1 teaspoon baking powder
1 teaspoon baking soda
½ teaspoon salt
2 eggs, beaten
2 cups buttermilk
2 tablespoons melted unsalted butter

In a bowl, sift together the dry ingredients. Add the eggs, buttermilk, and butter and stir just to mix. The batter will be lumpy.

Place a griddle or skillet over moderately high heat to get hot. Test by scattering a few drops of water on the surface. If the drops dance and sputter, the pan is hot enough. Grease the surface lightly with butter. Ladle about 3 circles of batter into the pan and cook until bubbles appear on the uncooked side, 3 to 4 minutes. Turn the flapjacks and cook until lightly browned, 2 to 3 minutes more. Serve with butter and molasses, honey, preserves, maple syrup, or my Caramel Syrup (page 46).

MAKES ABOUT A DOZEN 4-INCH FLAPJACKS

I f I had a nickel for every batch of buttermilk biscuits I've made in my lifetime, I'd be the wealthiest person around! Instead, I am rich with family and friends. Try these biscuits hot from the oven with lots of butter and a dab of homemade preserves or Hot Pepper Jelly (page 22).

2 cups sifted all-purpose flour
2 teaspoons baking powder
1 teaspoon sugar
1 teaspoon salt
½ teaspoon baking soda
5 tablespoons unsalted butter
¾ cup buttermilk

Preheat the oven to 450°.

In a bowl, combine the flour, baking powder, sugar, salt, and baking soda. Using a pastry blender, cut in the butter until the mixture resembles coarse meal. Make a well in the center and add the buttermilk. Stir quickly and lightly to incorporate the dry ingredients.

Flour a pastry board and knead the dough for a few seconds. Pat or roll out the dough until it is about ¼ inch thick. Use a 2-inch round cutter and place the biscuits on an ungreased baking sheet. Bake for 10 to 12 minutes, until lightly browned.

MAKES ABOUT 20 2-INCH BISCUITS

PECAN CORN MUFFINS

These muffins use my favorite ingredients: nuts and cornmeal. They're awfully good spread with some whipped honey butter right after I take them from the oven.

1¼ cups yellow cornmeal
1 cup sugar
¾ cup all-purpose flour
2 teaspoons baking powder
¼ teaspoon salt
1 cup chopped pecans
1 cup milk
8 tablespoons (1 stick) unsalted butter, melted
2 eggs, beaten

Preheat the oven to 425°. Generously butter a muffin tin.

In a bowl, combine the cornmeal, sugar, flour, baking powder, and salt. Stir in the pecans.

In another bowl, combine the milk, butter, and eggs. Quickly beat the liquids into the dry ingredients, stirring briefly, just to mix. Pour into the muffin cups and bake until browned, about 15 minutes.

MAKES 1½ DOZEN

Use whatever type of pear suits your fancy. I like Seckels, Bartletts, Comices, and Boscs. Top this cake with Spicy Rum-Butter Sauce (page 43), Brandy Sauce (page 44), or a dollop of Peach and Pecan Conserve (page 30).

4 *cups grated pears*
2 *cups sugar*
1 *cup chopped pecan pieces*
1 *cup vegetable oil*
1 *teaspoon vanilla extract*
2 *eggs, beaten*
3 *cups all-purpose flour*
½ *teaspoon salt*
2 *teaspoons baking soda*
½ *teaspoon ground cinnamon or freshly grated nutmeg*

In a large bowl, combine the pears, sugar, and pecans. Set aside for 1 hour to accumulate juice.

Preheat the oven to 350°. Butter and flour a large tube pan.

Using a wooden spoon, stir into the pear mixture the oil, vanilla, and eggs. Stirring by hand, add the remaining dry ingredients. Do not use a mixer. Pour the batter into the prepared tube pan and bake for 1 hour and 15 minutes, until a broom straw or toothpick inserted in the center comes out clean.

SERVES 16

HOMEMADE VANILLA ICE CREAM

This ice cream is addictive—you just can't stop eating it. Let your imagination go and think of all the good things you could add to it when it's about half frozen. I'm partial to adding chunks of fresh peaches or figs. Top with Creamy Caramel Sauce (page 47), Brandy Sauce (page 44), Praline Sauce (page 45), or any homemade preserves.

    2 quarts milk
 1½ cups sugar
       Pinch of salt
    6 eggs, well beaten
    2 tablespoons vanilla extract
    1 13-ounce can evaporated milk,
       chilled in the freezer

In a heavy pot, scald the milk over low heat. Add the sugar and salt and stir to dissolve. Add the eggs, a little at a time, and stir in the vanilla. Cook, stirring, over low heat until the mixture thickens enough to coat a spoon.

Whip the cold evaporated milk just as you would heavy cream and add it to the custard. Chill the mixture for several hours before freezing in an ice-cream maker according to the manufacturer's directions.

MAKES 3 TO 4 QUARTS

When I was a little girl, my mother used to make this gingerbread on our wooden stove—the whole house smelled of it. It was wonderful. In cold weather she sometimes added golden raisins to make it even better. Try it right from the oven topped with Brandy Sauce (page 44), Spicy Rum-Butter Sauce (page 43), Homemade Ice Cream (page 66), or flavored whipped cream. Hmmm!

½ *cup sugar*
8 *tablespoons (1 stick) unsalted butter, softened*
2 *eggs, beaten*
½ *cup molasses*
2½ *cups sifted all-purpose flour*
1 *teaspoon ground cinnamon*
½ *teaspoon ground cloves*
1 *teaspoon ground ginger*
1 *teaspoon salt*
1 *teaspoon baking soda*
1 *cup boiling water*
1 *cup golden raisins (optional)*

Preheat the oven to 325°. Butter a 13 × 8-inch pan.

In a bowl, cream together the sugar and butter. Stir in the eggs, molasses, flour, spices, salt, soda, and boiling water (and raisins, if you are using them).

Pour the mixture into the prepared pan and bake for 35 minutes, or until the top springs back when touched (the raisins might extend the baking time).

SERVES 8

I love the late afternoon light in the small sitting room of the house.

Pantry Bonus: Tinned Treats

CREOLE PRALINES

Of all the specialties from this part of the country, I suppose that pralines are the most well-known sweet. These are easy to make and delicious to eat. I keep them in an airtight tin and give them to my great-granddaughter for an occasional treat.

2 *cups granulated sugar*
1 *cup tightly packed dark brown sugar*
8 *tablespoons (1 stick) unsalted butter*
1 *cup milk*
2 *teaspoons light Karo syrup*
4 *cups pecan halves or pieces*

In a medium saucepan, bring the sugars, butter, milk, and syrup to the boil over moderate heat. Cook over low heat for 20 minutes. Stir in the pecans and cook until the mixture forms a soft ball when dropped into cold water. Stir well and drop by spoonfuls onto waxed paper. Cool and wrap in individual squares of waxed paper.

MAKES ABOUT 2½ DOZEN

OLD-FASHIONED TEA CAKES

There are lots of sweet confections you can make and keep in tightly sealed tins on the pantry shelf. These tea cakes take me back to my childhood, when my mother used to make them once a week. They keep very well. My great-granddaughter Leanne loves them just as much as I did when I was her age.

1 *pound (4 sticks) unsalted butter*
1½ *cups sugar*
1 *whole egg plus 1 egg yolk*
5 *cups all-purpose flour*
1 *teaspoon vanilla extract*
½ *teaspoon salt*

In a large bowl, cream together the butter and sugar. Stir in the whole egg and the egg yolk and add the flour, vanilla, and salt. Mix well and shape the dough into a ball. Wrap the dough in plastic and chill it for at least 1 hour or for a day or two before baking.

Preheat the oven to 350°.

On a lightly floured board, roll out the dough until it is about ¼-inch thick. Cut out tea cakes with a plain or fancy 2-inch cutter. Place on ungreased baking sheets and bake until lightly browned, about 8 to 10 minutes. Watch closely, as these tea cakes burn easily.

MAKES ABOUT 5 DOZEN

MOLASSES POPCORN BALLS

These really take me back to Christmases past. When my daughter, Freddie, and her cousin, Lee, were young, I used to wrap these popcorn balls in red or green cellophane and put them under the Christmas tree. They made a nice little holiday treat for the children and for people who came to call.

1 cup sugar
1 tablespoon distilled white vinegar
2 tablespoons molasses
1 tablespoon unsalted butter
½ teaspoon salt
6 to 8 cups popped popcorn

In a large saucepan, bring the sugar, vinegar, and ½ cup water to the boil over moderate heat. Cook for 5 minutes.

Add the molasses, butter, and salt and cook until a few drops become hard and brittle when dropped into cold water. Remove from the heat and stir in the popcorn.

Working quickly—you might want to butter your fingers so you can handle the stuff—shape the popcorn into balls. Wrap in waxed paper or cellophane and store in an airtight container.

MAKES 6 TO 8 LARGE BALLS OR ABOUT 15 SMALL BALLS

These strawberry confections make a nice light dessert for a midsummer dinner served outside, just before the lightning bugs come out. The meringues can be prepared ahead and stored airtight in a tin on the pantry shelf. If the humidity is high, the meringues might not work—better make ice cream instead.

> 4 *egg whites, at room temperature*
> ½ *teaspoon cream of tartar*
> 1 *cup sugar*
> 1 *cup fresh strawberries*
> ½ *cup strawberry preserves, diluted with*
>   *2 tablespoons hot water*
>   *Whipped cream (optional)*

Preheat the oven to 250°. Line a baking sheet with brown paper.

In a deep bowl, beat the egg whites with the cream of tartar until very stiff. Beating constantly, add the sugar, 1 tablespoon at a time. Pipe or spoon small "nests" of meringue onto the baking sheet. Sprinkle lightly with sugar and bake for 1 hour. Turn off the heat, but leave the meringues in the closed oven for 1 to 1½ hours more.

To serve, fill the meringues with fresh berries and drizzle the preserves over them. Top with whipped cream and a perfect strawberry.

MAKES ABOUT 12 MERINGUES

Index